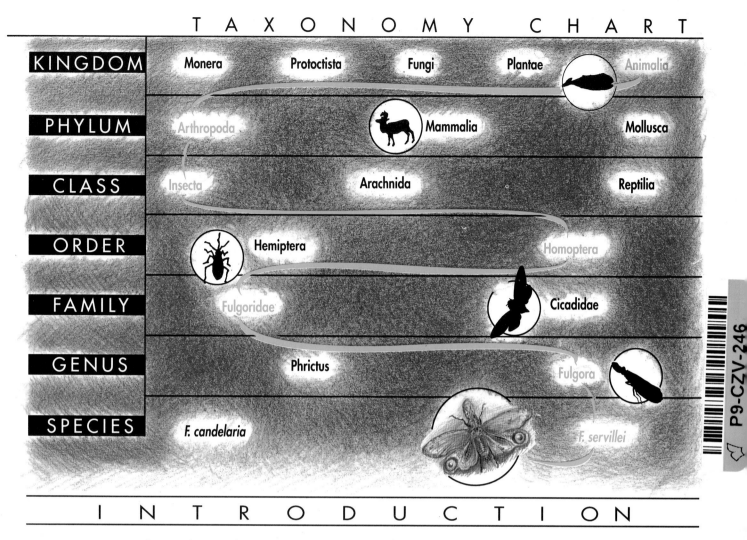

KINGDOM	Monera	Protoctista	Fungi	Plantae	Animalia

PHYLUM — Arthropoda, Mammalia, Mollusca

CLASS — Insecta, Arachnida, Reptilia

ORDER — Hemiptera, Homoptera

FAMILY — Fulgoridae, Cicadidae

GENUS — Phrictus, Fulgora

SPECIES — F. candelaria, F. servillei

P9-CZV-246

I N T R O D U C T I O N

Insects are everywhere! These adaptable animals thrive on land, in the air, and even under water. In fact, insects are the largest and most successful group of critters in the animal kingdom.

Insects are invertebrates, which means they don't have backbones (unlike mammals and most fishes, for instance). They belong to a large group of invertebrates called arthropods because of their jointed legs and their hard outer covering, or exoskeleton. Spiders, scorpions, centipedes, and crustaceans are arthropods, too. But insects can be distinguished from all other animals because their body has three parts (head, thorax, and abdomen), they have six legs, and they often have wings.

Insects are divided into five main groups—beetles, bugs, flies, wasps (including ants and bees), and butterflies (and moths). There are at least fifteen smaller groups that include cockroaches, mantids, grass-hoppers, dragonflies, stick insects, lice, and fleas.

Although humans classify many insects as pests, these small animals play a vital role in maintaining the balance of nature. They carry pollen from one plant to another, ensuring future seeds and fruit. They recycle dead plants and animals back into the earth. Some are predators who help keep prey populations under control. And they are a key source of food for birds, fish, and small mammals. Without invertebrates such as insects, many other living things would not survive.

More than 780,000 species of insects have been named so far. Entomologists (scientists who study insects) guess there are many more that haven't been discovered yet!

Entomologists and other scientists use a universal system to keep track of insects and the millions of animal and plant species on earth. That system is called taxonomy, and it starts with the 5 main (or broadest) groups of all living things, the kingdoms. It then divides those into the next groups down—phylum, then class, order, family, genus, and, finally, species. Members of a *species* look similar, and they can reproduce with each other.

For an example of how taxonomy works, follow the highlighted lines above to see how the peanut-head bug (*Fulgora servillei*) is classified. In this book, the scientific name of each insect is listed next to the common name. In some cases, only the family name is used.

Turn to the glossarized index if you're looking for a specific insect, or for special information (what are compound eyes, for instance), or for the definition of a word you don't understand.

NET-WINGED BEETLE (*Lycus* sp.)

The net-winged beetle flies very slowly and clumsily, so it can't depend on a quick getaway to avoid predators. Instead, its body fluids are so bad-tasting and bitter that predators, warned by its bright colors and patterns, sometimes stay away.

Net-winged beetles have soft bodies and leathery-looking front wings. Usually, each wing is wide at the tip and narrow at the base. Often, their head lengthens into a beak, and their bodies have bright yellow and black bands, stripes, or spots that make them hard to miss as they cling to plants and flowers.

MARY SUNDSTROM

There are about 3,000 species of net-winged beetles. They live mostly in tropical areas. They hunt for snails and insects and, in turn, are hunted by birds and monkeys.

BETH EVANS

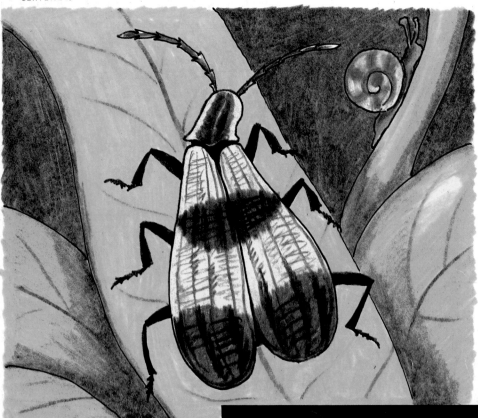

Beetles, frogs, fishes, and many other animals depend on brightly colored bodies to warn predators to stay away! Predators learn quickly to connect bright warning colors with a very yucky taste.

Copy moths! Some species of moths have evolved into almost perfect mimics of net-winged beetles. Since they sport the same bright warning colors and patterns of the bad-tasting beetles, predators avoid them.

What's so special about a beetle? For one thing, a beetle boasts a pair of tough front wings (elytra) that protect the delicate hind wings folded underneath. A beetle's skeleton is sturdier than that of many insects; and its primitive mouthparts are able to chew solid food.

Photo, facing page, courtesy Animals Animals © Michael Fogden

INSECTS

BRUSH-SNOUTED WEEVIL (*Rhina barbirostris*)

Weevils are beetles with very long heads, and their eyes, elbowed antennae, and mouthparts are set far apart from each other. The family known as true weevils (numbering at least 50,000 species) is the largest in the entire animal kingdom. True weevils are sometimes called snout beetles, elephant beetles, and billbugs because most sport an extremely long proboscis, or snout.

True weevils are herbivores (they feed only on plants), and they live all over the world. They have a reputation as pests because they often bore into wood, leaves, seeds, and other plant tissue.

The brush-snouted weevil is a large beetle from South America and Trinidad. It is also called the palm weevil because its larvae burrow into the trunks of coconut palms, killing the trees. Like many other animals, true weevils are most numerous in warmer regions of the world.

Biting jaws at the very tip of the weevil's snout (rostrum) are used to chomp down, while the snout itself is a drilling tool. The snout-weevil's antennae elbow out from either side of the snout. At each antenna's tip, a "hairy" club allows the weevil to sense the plant seed or stem surface into which it is drilling.

The largest true weevils reach a length of three inches, but on the average, they are less than one-fourth of an inch.

Photo, facing page, courtesy Animals Animals © Michael Fogden

INSECTS

COCKCHAFER BEETLE (*Melolontha melolontha*)

Insects were the first animals to master flight. Airborne travel gave them the chance to escape predators and to journey in search of food. Like the prehistoric ancestors of birds, primitive wingless insects may have first used basic flaps to glide from plant to plant. Eventually, the flaps evolved into wings. Fossil records prove the earliest known flying insects had two pairs of flapping wings that did not fold. Today, some insects still have nonfolding wings. Others (such as butterflies and wasps) depend on linked front and hind wings for greater flight efficiency.

Just like the pilot of an airliner, the cockchafer beetle prepares for takeoff with a "safety check." The beetle opens and closes its tough front wings (elytra) two or three times to make sure they are working smoothly. As takeoff proceeds, the cockchafer spreads its front wings while both antennae are widened to test which way the wind is blowing. When the front wings are fully extended to each side, the hind wings unfold automatically and the beetle springs upward. Liftoff! In flight, the beating hind wings provide the power stroke, while the elytra offer some aerodynamic lift.

Wings are great for flight, but that's not all. Insects use their wings—brightly colored, perfumed, or noisy—to attract a mate.

Muscles located in the cockchafer's thorax provide power for flap-flap-flapping wings. When vertical and horizontal muscles tighten alternately, the wings raise and lower.

North American cockchafer beetles are easy to find in May and June when they bang and buzz against window and door screens.

Photo, facing page, courtesy Animals Animals © Michael Fogden

INSECTS

PEANUT-HEAD BUG (*Fulgora servillei*)

The bulbous peanut-head bug has an eye-catching way to frighten hungry predators. It depends on an extra set of very large eyespots located on its hind wings. When the peanut-head bug opens its wings and flashes its giant "eyes," it buys time to escape from a predator who might mistake the "eyes" for those of its own enemies.

The peanut-head bug is a member of the fulgorid group, or the "lantern flies." *Fulgor* is Latin for "flash of lightning," but the name is based on folklore. People used to believe that the large head of a fulgorid would glow in the dark like a lantern; now scientists have proved it to be a no glow.

Even though they don't shine in the dark, there is no denying fulgorids are extremely weird. They often sport nifty colors, and they always have huge heads! They live in Mexico, Central America, and other tropical regions where they feed on plant juices.

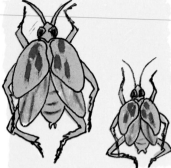

True bugs belong to the order Hemiptera (he-MIP-te-rah); that is, their hind wings are thin and clear, and their front wings are thick at the base but thin at the tip. True bugs have a life cycle that includes incomplete metamorphosis; the young nymphs look and act much like the adult bug.

Instead of two pairs of wings, flies have one wing pair and nubby balancing organs (halteres). These help the fly control roll, pitch, and yaw and land upside down. They act a bit like a fly gyroscope.

INSECTS

HARLEQUIN BUG (*Tectocoris diophthalmus*)

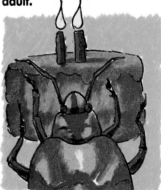

Most insects hatch from eggs; while some emerge as larvae (caterpillars, maggots, or grubs), others look almost like adults of their species. If they also grow up without going through a pupal (resting) stage, their life cycle involves *incomplete* metamorphosis. Harlequin bugs change markings slightly as they pass from egg to young nymph (see facing page) and later nymph stages, but basically, they look much the same as when they hatched.

The most advanced insects have a life cycle that includes *complete* metamorphosis. Metamorphosis means change of body form, and stages of complete metamorphosis—egg, larvae, and adult—all are distinct from each other.

In complete metamorphosis, a larva emerges from its egg with simple eyes and a soft body that hardens quickly. A larva will often devour its egg shell, consuming important minerals, before it searches for other food. After it has grown and molted (shed) its cuticle, or skin, the larva will attach itself to a leaf and begin to pupate. For the final time, the larval cuticle is shed, and the exposed pupal cuticle hardens immediately.

During the pupal stage, the insect's entire body is re-formed. Nerves and muscles dissolve, and new ones are created. When this process is complete, the young adult insect slowly emerges from a split in the pupal skin.

It may take several hours before the newly free adult insect is able to travel. During this time, it is very vulnerable to predators. Surviving insects may not develop their full color markings for more than a week.

This harlequin bug is a nymph. In Greek and Roman mythology, a nymph is a nature goddess. In entomology (the study of insects), a nymph is the young of any insect whose life cycle does not include complete metamorphosis. It is also another name for a pupa, which is an insect in the stage of development between larva and adult.

Photo, facing page, courtesy Animals Animals © Kathie Atkinson/OSF

Most insects have a life cycle of only one year, but some may live for two or more (especially in temperate climates). They may spend the winter as a nymph or pupa, becoming an adult the following spring or summer.

INSECTS

SHIELD STINKBUG (*Lyramorpha* sp.)

Stinkbugs are just that—stinky. They discharge a smelly liquid from two pores on their underside when they're disturbed. This is a good way of keeping hungry predators—who don't want a stinky mouthful—at bay.

Stinkbugs can be recognized by their very broad, convex bodies that are often brown or metallic. Some species are more colorful and sport shades of red, orange, black, or blue in assorted patterns.

Stinkbugs are also known as shield bugs because they have a scutellum, or shield, that covers the hind part of their body. Sometimes the female uses it to shield her eggs and young when she sits over them. The stinkbugs pictured here are nymphs, which means they are not yet fully mature. They look much like adult stinkbugs of their genus. These stinkbugs live in Australia.

A few of the 5,000 or so known species of stinkbugs prey on other insects, but most feed on fruit juices. People often consider stinkbugs pests because they damage fruits, vegetables, and other plants as they feed. The problem is greatest when a species overpopulates, but as farmers and gardeners learn more about insects, they are finding ways to control pest populations without the use of poisonous pesticides.

Bombardier beetles blast curious predators with a noisy jet of boiling chemicals fired from the rear. Some species spray in speedy spurts—500 per second! Two chemicals—stored in the beetle's abdomen—mix when fired, and the result repels predators such as spiders, birds, frogs, mice, and ants.

One Asian stinkbug can squirt its smelly secretions for a distance of 12 inches, and it makes a loud noise at the same time!

14

INSECTS

Photo, facing page, courtesy Animals Animals © K. G. Preston-Mafham

BEE BEETLE (*Trichius fasciatus*)

The bee beetle belongs to the scientific family Passalidae, commonly known as the betsy beetles. There are about 500 species, who inhabit mostly tropical areas of Asia and Central America. Only four species of betsy beetles are found in North America.

While most betsy beetles are large and have powerful jaws and a small horn on their head, the bee beetle is among the smallest of this group. It looks a lot like a small bee, which probably helps it discourage hungry predators. Bee beetles aren't the only bee mimics. Many other insects use "bee camouflage" to protect themselves.

Family groups of adult and larval betsy beetles live together in rotting logs, and they have a definite social structure. Even though it is primitive, the social behavior of this insect family is extremely unusual in beetles.

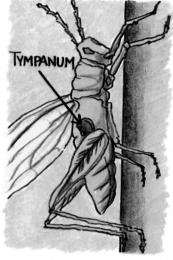

TYMPANUM

Say what? An extremely delicate built-in drum (tympanum) allows an insect to hear. This membrane is connected to special internal organs; they, in turn, carry impulses to the insect's brain. Depending on the critter, tympana may be located on an insect's antennae, knees, or abdomen.

More than 2,500 years ago, Egyptians tended bees in hives.

Bee scout! Honeybees are social critters. A bee scout who has found nectar will fly back to the hive and tell other bees where to find it. The bee communicates by dancing, and its directions are keyed off the sun. As the day passes, and the sun moves in the sky, the bee adjusts its dance accordingly.

Photo, facing page, courtesy Animals Animals © K. G. Preston-Mafham

16

INSECTS

HORSEFLY (*Chrysops* sp.)

Although horseflies look as if they are wearing great sunglasses, those shades are actually eyes—compound eyes, that is. Most insects have compound eyes that are made up of hundreds of simple eyes placed together. Each simple eye—really designed to detect motion and light—"sees" only a part of the picture. It's up to the insect's brain to piece together the pictures like a jigsaw puzzle.

Typically, insects have two very large compound eyes located toward the front and sides of their head and three simple eyes (called ocelli) on top. What would you see if you looked through an insect's eyes? Scientists know that a bee on a flower can see an animal move several yards away. But does the bee know whether the animal is a horse or a dog, or is it just a moving shape? Lots of insects see colors. (Bees and butterflies see a broader spectrum than we do!) But are beetles color-blind? Probably. If you study insects and their senses, you might be able to answer these questions some day.

All 2,500 species of horseflies have compound eyes. In males, these eyes take up most of the surface of the head. *Chrysops*, and many other species, boast an especially beautiful rainbow of iridescent hues that band or spot the eyes.

Horseflies can be as small as a house fly or as long as more than an inch. Female horseflies are pesky critters because they feed on the blood of other animals, including humans. They cut through a victim's skin using their short, sharp mouthparts, and then they lap up flowing blood. Horseflies rarely transmit diseases that affect humans, but they do carry some animal diseases.

How touching. Insects depend on thousands of sensory hairs fringing the surface of their body to tell them what's what. These hairs are connected to nerve endings. When an insect moves its leg, it also moves its leg hairs. Then, the insect's brain receives the message that its leg is bent.

Some horseflies (such as *Chrysops*) are also known as deer flies and moose flies because they prey on you know who. Because common names vary so much from place to place, scientists give each plant and animal a scientific name that is used the world over.

Photo, facing page, courtesy Animals Animals © Stephen Dalton/OSF

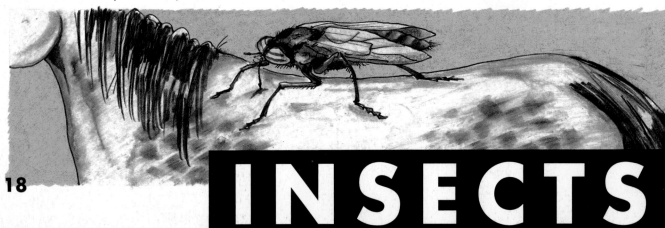

INSECTS

BULLDOG ANT (*Myrmecia gulosa*)

Wasps, ants, and bees, and their relatives, belong to one of the biggest insect groups in the world. There are at least 200,000 known species, and more are discovered each year.

It's easy to spot a member of this group: look for a very narrow waist where the thorax and the abdomen meet. But watch out for the stinger of many female bees, wasps, and ants. The ovipositor (egg-laying organ) at the tip of the female's abdomen can inflict a painful sting, which is used in self-defense.

In addition to a stinger, many ants have fierce jaws that may inflict a painful bite. Members of some species are also able to shoot formic acid from their abdomen as they bite so their unfortunate victim feels double the pain!

The most primitive (those who closely resemble their ancestors) of all ants belong to a subfamily called Ponerinae. The ponerines are the largest, most colorful, and most aggressive of living ants. They include bulldog ants, most of which are inhabitants of Australia.

There are about 100 species of bulldog ants; these impressively large ants may reach a length of one inch (about 25 mm). In addition, they are feared for their aggressive nature and extremely painful sting. This they inflict with a stinger that is one quarter of an inch long. Although many species of ants live in huge colonies of 100,000 individuals, only a few thousand bulldog ants will live together in simple earth nests underground.

Bulldog ants are nimble hunters who prey mostly on insects and spiders, which are fed to the larvae. Adults also have a sweet tooth for the juice of plants. Bulldog ants are pugnacious and will attack anything that disturbs their nest, including humans. They have been known to pursue people for 30 feet, and besides being swift runners, some can leap several inches.

Ants often live in huge colonies (with 100,000 individuals!) in which they communicate by smell and touch.

INSECTS

GULF FRITILLARY BUTTERFLY (*Agraulis vanillae*)

The gulf fritillary (also known as the silver-spotted flambeau) lives in Central and South America. The adult is famous for the beautiful silver patches on the underside of its hind wing.

In its larval stage—as a caterpillar—the gulf fritillary feeds on the leaves of passion flowers. It is protected from some predators, such as birds, by its extremely stiff and sticky barbed spines. Unfortunately, even the stickiest spines are no protection against predatory wasps. After one sting, the wasp deposits its egg in the paralyzed body of the caterpillar. When the wasp larva hatches, it feeds on the flesh of its host.

Adult fritillaries (and all other butterflies) feed on liquid nectar that they suck in through their extremely long proboscis, or tube-shaped feeding organ. When it's not at work, the butterfly's proboscis curls up for handy storage.

A butterfly's body is covered with tiny scales that seem to "know" which way the wings fold after flight.

Butterflies probably acquired their name when common yellow butterflies reminded someone of flying butter.

Insects rely on keen taste organs located around their jaw. Some insects "feel" taste using their antennae. Some butterflies have taste organs on their feet; these are so sensitive, the butterfly's proboscis automatically uncoils at the first touch of a tasty flower.

INSECTS

DEATH'S-HEAD SPHINX (*Acherontia atropos*)

Like all members of its family, the death's-head sphinx moth is such a powerful flyer, its beating wings seem to disappear in a blur. But when it comes to travel and feeding, this moth is the exception, not the rule.

Most sphinx moths fly from flower to flower feeding on nectar with their extremely long proboscis, but the death's-head sphinx uses its short tongue to pierce honeycomb in beehives and suck honey. Sphinx moths hardly ever travel long distances, but the death's-head sphinx regularly migrates from Africa to northern Europe.

This moth earned its named because of the pattern on its thorax that resembles a human skull, but sphinx moths as a group are named for a habit they have as caterpillars. While resting, the caterpillars assume a peculiar position—head curved down below their thorax and the front part of their body raised—which is much like the posture of the Egyptian sphinx. The entire caterpillar looks like the front end of a very large—and very frightening—animal. This defensive, or threat, posture is an effective way to scare away hungry predators.

It is easy to mistake sphinx moths for hummingbirds because they have a large body and a habit of hovering in front of a flower while they feed.

A tropical sphinx moth, *Erinnyis ello*, regularly commutes all the way from South America to Canada.

Handy wipes! Some butterflies use their two front legs to clean their eyes. They let their other four legs do the walking.

Photo, facing page, courtesy Animals Animals © Alistair Shay/OSF

INSECTS

FLAT-FACED KATYDID (*Lirometopum coronatum*)

Male katydids make music by winging it. One forewing is equipped with a file that is rubbed against a scraper on the other forewing. The sound is made louder when the katydid raises its forewings slightly to create a small resonant cavity, or "mini speaker."

Katydids, grasshoppers, crickets, and mole-crickets belong to the scientific order Orthoptera, which means "straight wing." All males of this order "sing" to attract a mate; both males and females have excellent hearing. (In a few species, females are also capable of singing.) The katydid's tympana (eardrums) are located on its front legs, just about where you would find your kneecap.

Most members of the Orthoptera can fly, although jumping—powered by their long, strong hind legs—is their preferred method of locomotion. If you've ever tried to catch a katydid, you know what excellent jumpers they really are!

Some katydids have an extremely weird way of defending themselves from predators; it's called "reflex bleeding." Blood flows from the thorax or is squirted from the first joint of the leg. Certain species aim with great accuracy and always hit the bull's-eye.

Locusts are famous for swarming. On each major continent, there exist one or more species of locusts prone to population explosions. When this happens, millions of these locusts travel in mind-boggling swarms, and they may devour *all* vegetation in their path. Even the Bible mentions a plague of locusts.

Photo, facing page, courtesy Animals Animals © Michael Fogden

INSECTS

CRYPTIC MANTIS (*Choeradolis* sp.)

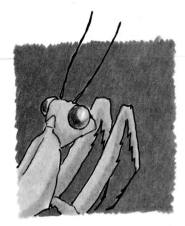

Praying mantises are named for their posture at rest; their front legs are folded and zipped together by interlocking spines into a "praying" position.

Mantis is Greek for "soothsayer" or "prophet," and it is the name given this insect group by Swedish naturalist Carolus Linnaeus who lived in the eighteenth century. Although mantids look very wise and saintly, they are fierce predators who use their "praying arms" to lash out and impale their victims. Mantids depend on excellent eyesight to spot prey, and they are able to attack with great speed. They feed on insects (often other mantids) and other invertebrates as well as frogs, lizards, and small birds. Mantids don't go in search of prey. Instead, they lie in ambush.

Most of the 1,800 mantid species depend on camouflage to surprise their victims. Because their wings are patterned with leaflike designs and their limbs are long and twiglike, they are able to blend in with their background. Some even mimic bark and tree moss. Depending on the species, mantids come in a variety of lengths, from one to five inches.

Mantids are very easy to recognize because they have a movable head, a slender body, and prehensile legs (the better to grasp their prey). They lay their eggs in foamy, papery egg capsules. Each capsule may contain 200 eggs, and a female might produce as many as five capsules each year. Although the eggs are deposited in the fall, they do not hatch until the following spring. The cryptic mantis (and most mantids) prefers warm or tropical climates.

In African folklore, mantids are sometimes used to represent spirits and gods.

Mantids and cockroaches are related, but cockroaches are nocturnal (active at night) herbivores while mantids are diurnal (active in the day) predators.

Photo, facing page, courtesy Animals Animals © G. I. Bernard

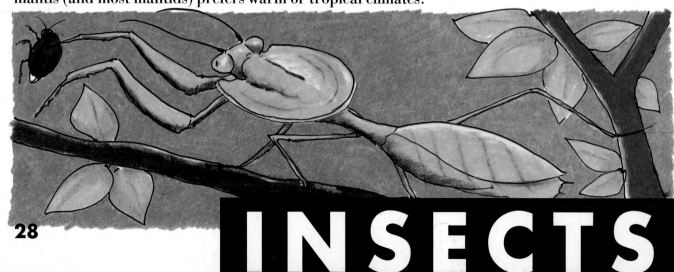

INSECTS

GIANT AUSTRALIAN STICK (*Extatosoma tiaratum*)

Walkingsticks and leaf insects all belong to the same scientific family: Phasmidae. As a group, they live mostly in the tropical areas of Asia, although some species have been seen as far north as Europe and North America. Members of this family come in a variety of shapes and colors, and they may resemble green, brown, or rotting leaves, thorns, grass, broken sticks, or stout twigs. One thing they all have in common is camouflage.

Many animals depend on a disguise—protective coloring or shape—to blend in with their background and to hide from predators. Camouflage is especially important for those animals that are not swift in the air or on the ground (a must for quick getaways) or who can't depend on other equipment—poison or armor, for instance—to keep danger away.

During the day, most stick and leaf insects stay almost completely motionless—in strange postures—made invisible by their resemblance to the plants and trees around them. Only the most alert bird or lizard can detect them in the stillness of daylight. They are most active under the cover of darkness, which is when they eat, mate, and drop their eggs.

Leaf insects have wings, but many species of stick insects do not. The giant Australian stick insect lives in Australia, of course.

Scent sense. Most insects have a sharp sense of smell. Some secrete smelly substances to ward off predators or attract mates.

Some of the Asian sticks qualify as the longest insects in the world. They reach a total length of more than one foot!

Photo, facing page, courtesy Animals Animals © R. H. Armstrong

INSECTS

MALAYAN LEAF INSECT (*Phyllium pulchrifolium*)

Huge Malayan leaf insects have wings and legs, and the sides of their body are flat and uneven like the edges of a leaf. To make matters even leafier, they are green, yellow, or brown.

During the day, they hang motionless, almost in a trance. When they do move, it is in slow motion, and they look like leaves blowing gently in the wind. Leaf insects have a special reflex action known as thanatosis, or playing dead. When they are startled, they automatically drop from their perch and stay perfectly still wherever they land.

Female leaf insects are flightless; they have lost their hind wings, although they do have leaflike front wings. Males *do* fly and are usually much smaller than females. The record length of a stick insect is 13 inches, but most are from 1 to 5 inches long.

All stick and leaf insects are herbivores (or plant eaters). Some species may reproduce in such numbers they can strip large areas of woodland. Commonly, they reproduce by parthenogenesis, which means the eggs are not fertilized by the male and develop into more females.

Malayan leaf insects of the genus Phyllium live in Malaysia and other areas of tropical Asia and Indonesia.

Walkingsticks, like leaf insects, depend on camouflage for protection from predators; they mimic the sticks around them. Some walkingsticks can stay still for more than 6 hours at a time!

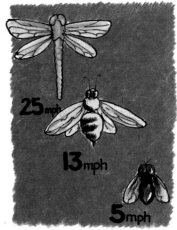

Call me speedy! Hawkmoths and dragonflies are the race cars of insects; they commonly cruise at 25 mph. Honeybees clock in at about 13 mph, butterflies at 12 mph, and house flies reach a slowpoke cruising speed of only 5 mph. And we still can't catch them!

Photo, facing page, courtesy Animals Animals © E. R. Degginger

INSECTS

DEWEY GREEN DARNER (*Anax junius*)

Darners are large, brightly colored dragonflies. Like all members of their family, they have a stout body, a large, movable head, and two pairs of large veiny wings. They also boast huge compound eyes (some can see in almost all directions at once, the better to spot their prey) and have biting and chewing mouthparts.

Dragonflies are fierce predators, and they pursue their prey—mosquitoes, flies, and gnats—on the wing. In flight, their bristly legs are used to clutch their victims while their long wings keep them airborne.

Skimmers are big colorful dragonflies often seen skimming shallow water or "sitting guard" on plants. They protect their territory from other dragonflies.

Dragonflies usually prefer habitats close to streams, lakes, and other permanent water sources. They need fresh water, in which their eggs hatch and the young reach maturity.

Dragonfly eggs are deposited in jellied masses that stick to water plants for several days. The newly hatched dragonfly nymph has no wings, and it may not mature for two or three years. During this immature stage of its life cycle, it lives completely underwater feeding on small fishes and tadpoles. When it grows large enough, the nymph crawls out of the water and molts to emerge as a fully winged dragonfly.

Darner species range from Alaska to Hawaii and the eastern coast of Asia. They are swift and graceful flyers whose wings are glassy; their abdomen is brilliant blue, and their brow is emerald green. Unlike most other dragonfies, adult darners can live far from water.

MMMMMM! Darners got their name because they were said to sew a child's mouth closed. But that's just a folktale!

To breathe underwater, the dewey green darner nymph uses internal gills that are in the form of ridges of tissue in its rectum. The nymph draws in and expels water across the ridges. If water is expelled very quickly, the nymph is jet propelled!

Photo, facing page, courtesy Animals Animals © John Gerlach

INSECTS

AMERICAN COCKROACH (*Periplaneta americana*)

Cockroaches; their primitive mouthparts are made for biting, and their long, slender legs are built for speed. The skittery sound of these pesky critters on the move is familiar to humans, because cockroaches have adapted to life most anywhere, especially in kitchens! Cockroaches are noisy on purpose; as they run, they drag the spurs at the ends of their legs on the ground to warn their fellows of danger. They may also produce smelly substances from their glands. Although they do have these warning signals, compared to many other insects, cockroaches are very primitive creatures.

Cockroaches are not very different from their fossilized ancestors. In fact, if you could travel back in time about 225 million years, you would probably see cockroaches (and other insects like dragonflies, leafhoppers, and cicadas) looking much as they do today. Cockroaches have stayed the same because they didn't *have* to change; they do an excellent job of surviving just as they are.

Like their ancestors, male cockroaches are winged. (In some species, both males and females sport wings.) The female cockroach produces two rows of eggs (a total of 30 or 40) inside a tough egg purse called an ootheca. She carries the purse on her abdomen until she finds a place to hide it. When the young are ready to hatch, they squeeze their way from the egg and through an opening in the purse.

The American cockroach lives in North America, but it originated in Africa. It grows to a length of about one inch (roughly 25 mm), which is small compared to its 3-inch-long tropical relatives.

Most insect fossils are of insect species who became extinct or evolved into different critters. Roaches and dragonflies are exceptions.

The first insect fossils date back about 345 million years and prove insects were living during the Carboniferous period. But entomologists know that insects have been around much longer than that because the fossils show many already distinctly different groups.

Fossils of the extremely large dragonfly *Meganeura monyi* show it had a wingspan of 3 feet!

Photo, facing page, courtesy Animals Animals © Bates Littlehales

INSECTS

Lousy Louse!

HUMAN HEAD LOUSE (*Pediculus humanus capitis*)

The human head louse belongs to a family of true (or sucking) lice that live and feed only on human primates. Besides the human head louse, humans also play host to the body louse (*Pediculus humanus humanus*). Other primates, such as chimpanzees and gorillas, host their own members of this true louse family.

True lice feed on blood that they draw from their host with their piercing and sucking mouthparts. They also need the vitamins they receive from the bacteria living inside their own miniscule bodies—which means there are parasites inside parasites. While the lice gain nutritional benefits, the bacteria live and breed inside *their* lice hosts. In fact, new generations of bacteria are transmitted to new generations of lice through the host eggs. In biology, this type of mutually beneficial living arrangement is known as symbiosis.

While human head lice live in hair, human body lice survive on clothing or bedding and jewelry and only climb onto the skin to move around.

Host with the most. If you are hosting lots of lice, it may be time to party down—down to the drugstore. Lice can make life extremely itchy and miserable.

Fleas are incredible athletes. A member of one tropical species can average one jump per second for as long as 72 hours if it is excited by nearby fleas.

Growing together. Primate lice are part of a recent family in evolutionary terms. They are developing only as quickly as their hosts—us primates—allow them to. As we evolve and change, so do they.

Photo, facing page, courtesy Animals Animals © Peter Parks/OSF

INSECTS

CICADA (Family Cicadidae)

Cicadas, aphids, and treehoppers all belong to the scientific order Homoptera, and they are different from true bugs (order Hemiptera) because their beak is attached to the very back of the head, and their two pairs of wings are both transparent membranes. (Bugs, in contrast, have a leathery base on their front wings, which is why they are known as "half wings," or Hemiptera.)

Members of Homoptera reproduce in a variety of ways depending on the species. Some reproduce sexually, and some may produce eggs that develop without being fertilized. Those that don't lay eggs give birth to live young. Although their methods differ, all homopterans are extremely prolific when it comes to reproduction.

Some species of cicadas may swarm by the thousands, and there are more than 1,500 species in the world. Their wide head, huge compound eyes, and three, small simple eyes, or ocelli, in between make them easy to recognize.

Most female cicadas are mute, but males are famous for their "songs." These are made by two drumlike membranes inside their abdomen. A muscle causes each membrane to change shape, and this, in turn, produces vibration and sound. The noise is made louder by an amplifying cavity near the drums. The males use their tunes to attract females at mating time. Although males have ears, these don't work when cicadas are making music. (Maybe this protects the cicadas from their own noise!) In a few species, females can make as much music as males.

The periodical cicada is famous for its 17-year life cycle. Females lay their eggs in trees, and the nymphs hatch in six weeks and drop to the ground where they burrow. They remain in the earth for 17 years, crawl to the surface, and leave their old cuticles behind. Within weeks, the adult cicadas have found a mate, laid their eggs, and died. There are 13-year cicadas also.

After cicadas, grasshoppers and crickets are the noisest insects. They make their music by several methods: rubbing the rough edges at the base of both front wings together; drawing their hind leg over their forewing; rubbing their femur over their abdomen; striking a hind wing on a forewing; or by opening and closing their hind wings very quickly. The resulting vibrations produce lots of noise. To pick up these noisy signals, long-horned grasshoppers and crickets have ears on their front legs that act as aerials.

Photo, facing page, courtesy Animals Animals © G. I. Bernard

INSECTS

HORNED TREEHOPPER (*Umbonia crassicornis*)

Treehoppers can be recognized by their unusual thorny or leaflike shape that is designed to match the thorny, leafy plants they live on. Their shape provides camouflage, allowing them to hide from potential predators.

Female treehoppers often cut two parallel slices into the bark of a tree and deposit their eggs inside. In some species, the females tend the eggs carefully.

Treehoppers and their close relatives, leafhoppers and spittlebugs, can best be recognized by their membranous wings that are raised rooflike over their body. They are all squatty and wedge-shaped, sporting short antennae and a small head, and they are known (and sometimes named) for their vigorous hopping ability.

Hoppers and spittlebugs are strict vegetarians who suck the juice from plants. To begin breaking down food before it reaches their stomach, they inject fluids into plants. These fluids are poisonous, and an infestation of treehoppers (or their kin) can cause stunted growth and discolored leaves on host plants.

In 335 B.C., Aristotle compiled the *Historia animalium*, which described at least 300 animals. In Italy, more than 400 years later, Pliny the Elder used that work to research his own 37-volume *Historia naturalis*. In addition to real animals, Pliny included mermaids, unicorns, and winged horses in his natural history.

Although they may be a gardener's foe, hoppers are fun to observe. Leafhoppers are often beautifully colored with bright yellow, red, green, and blue markings. Spittlebugs are less colorful and less energetic than hoppers when they are young. The horned treehopper lives in Florida and the New World tropics.

Photo, facing page, courtesy Animals Animals © John L. Pontier

INSECTS

APPLE APHID (*Aphis pomi*)

Tiny, pear-shaped aphids are mighty because of their great numbers and their ability to produce honeydew (a sweet substance secreted by some plant-eating insects). They are almost defenseless, but many species depend on ants to defend them. Ants "milk" the aphids for honeydew, and they also provide shelter for their charges, carry them from plant to plant, and attack predators.

Like other homopterans, aphids are amazingly prolific. If nothing interfered with reproduction, in only ten months, the offspring of a single female aphid would number about 210000000000000000000000000000000000000000000000000 00000000000000000000000000000000000000000000000000000 000. That's a lot of teeny critters.

In the fall, true male and female aphids mate and deposit their eggs, which survive through winter and hatch in the spring. Nymphs immediately begin to suck sap from the host plant (home base). They pile up in layers and feed in mass. They soon deposit their own eggs, which produce females only. During the warm summer season, many generations of "short-lived" females produce young without sexual reproduction. Only at the end of summer, when temperatures drop, do true males appear to mate with females.

Aphids may move to different host plants depending on which stage of their life cycle they are in. They are found worldwide. Apple aphids live on apple, pear, plum, and cherry trees.

Rainy day friends: Ants tending aphids will even carry their tiny charges into their own nests during rainy or cold weather.

Too much gall! Aphids can be great pests where humans are concerned. In 1860, an aphid was imported from America to Europe where it devastated 2.5 million acres of vines over a 25-year period. The aphids caused galls (tumors) on the roots of the vines.

Photo, facing page, courtesy Animals Animals © E. R. Degginger

INSECTS

This glossarized index will help you find specific information on insects. It will also help you understand the meaning of some of the words used in this book.

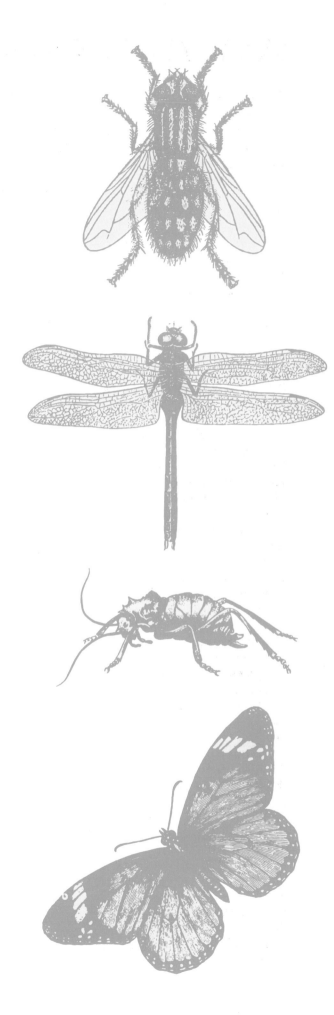